we ♥love♥ you...

Katy

An Unauthorised 2012 Annual

Written by Sarah Milne

Designed by Mathew Whittles

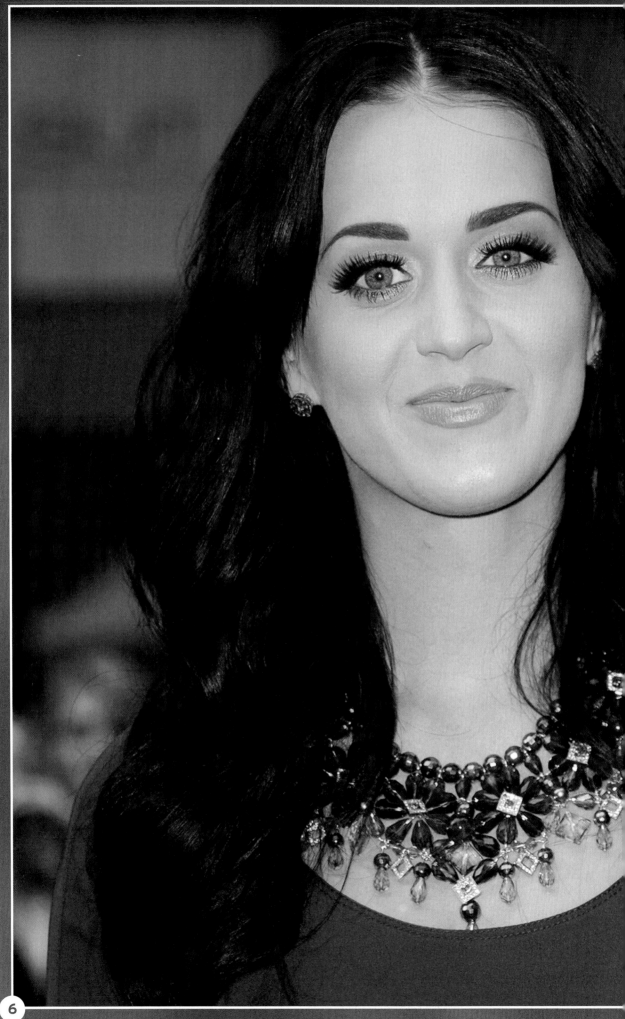

Contents

Teenage Dreams

Katheryn Elizabeth Hudson was born on October 25, 1984, to Keith and Mary, both pastors. Katy, as she is known, is the middle child - she has an older sister called Angela and a younger brother called David. She was born and raised in Santa Barbara in California

gospel

From the age of 9, Katy has both attended and sung at services in the church that her parents run. Katy's parents brought their children up in a Christian environment, going to church meetings and spending the holidays at Christian summer camps. The only music young Katy was allowed to listen to was gospel, and this is the style she first started singing, too. In fact she once got in trouble from her parents for singing Alanis Morissette in the playground.

tattoo

Katy took dance lessons, and started singing at home to copy her older sister. When her parents heard her they thought she should take singing lessons too and she started these at the age of nine.

Katy left school for a career in music, and at one time, she enrolled in a Music Academy in Santa Barbara to study Italian Opera!

Katy's early years were very important to her – she remains close to all her family members, and the values of her upbringing are always there. She has the word Jesus tattooed on her left wrist and it reminds her of her childhood.

When she was just 15 years old, some music executives spotted Katy's talents. She went to Nashville, Tennessee to start recording some demos, and all her Teenage Dreams started to come true...

Road to Success

At just 15 years old, Katy went to the home of country music, Nashville, Tennessee. Some professional musicians had heard her singing in church and took her there to help expand and develop her songwriting abilities. While Katy was there she started recording demos, and learning from the country music veterans - how to play guitar, the art of writing a song.

madonna

All this hard work obviously paid off, and Katy was first signed to the Christian record label, Red Hill, when she was still just 15, releasing her debut album (as Katy Hudson) in 2001. The gospel rock album wasn't that successful, and unfortunately, the label went bust at the end of the year,

Nashville

country music

Katy then decided to change her name to Katy Perry (Perry is her mother's maiden name), as her real name was too close to actress Kate Hudson's name, and she moved to Los Angeles to start a career in the music business. At 17, she started working on an album for Island records which was due to be released in 2005, but in the end it fizzled out and nothing happened.

Another disappointment for Katy, but she just kept on working, signing for Columbia records in 2004. Columbia didn't think she was a good front woman though, so instead asked her to work with producers The Matrix, as their female vocalist. This record company was also going to drop her, when someone from Virgin records saw her and finally recognised her talents. Katy signed with the Capitol Music group in 2007.

The hard work then started to ensure that Katy became the star she is today – lots of online marketing created a buzz round Katy, and even Madonna ended up talking about her on a radio show. I Kissed A Girl was finally released in 2008, and the rest is history...

KP fans

Katy is definitely an artist who appreciates and wants to interact with her fans as much as possible.

Always taking the time to give fans an autograph or have her picture taken with them, she's built up a loyal following of Katy lovers all over the world. She is an artist who seems to naturally bring together all types of people and we love her for that!

Here are a few pictures of Katy doing what she does best – being charming, friendly and open to her real fans everywhere.

Discography

Katy has certainly been a busy girl since her debut single, *I Kissed A Girl*, which was released in 2008. Here's a list of her major releases since then, and we're sure there's much more to come

2008

ALBUM
One of the Boys
Reached number 9 in the US and 11 in the UK charts. Went 2 x Platinum in Canada and Australia

SINGLES
I Kissed a Girl
7 x Platinum in Canada

Hot n Cold
6 x Platinum in Canada

2009

ALBUM
MTV Unplugged

SINGLES
Thinking of You
Platinum in Canada

Waking Up in Vegas
Platinum in Canada

2010

ALBUM
Teenage Dreams
Debuted at number 1 in US, Australia, Canada, Ireland, and UK. Went 2 x Platinum in Australia Canada, Ireland, UK and New Zealand

SINGLES
California Gurls
(featuring Snoop Dogg)
4 x Platinum in US, Australia and Canada

Teenage Dream
4 x Platinum in Australia

Firework
4 x Platinum in US, Australia and Canada

2011

SINGLES
E.T.
(featuring Kanye West)
4 x Platinum in US

Last Friday Night (T.G.I.F.)
Gold in Australia and New Zealand

Katy

Collaborations

With such a big variety of influences, Katy is always open to working with people from different styles of music, and that means lots of exciting collaborations.

Her first album, under her real name, was strictly a gospel album, but since then most of her work has had input from other people. When she was first signed to Columbia in 2004, they didn't think she had what it took to be a front woman, and instead paired her with record production team The Matrix, working on their album as the female vocalist.

Since releasing her first Katy Perry album though, Katy has chosen lots of exciting artists to work with, and these are some of our favourites:

snoop dogg

kanye west

timbaland

2008

Katy sang backing vocals on Bush frontman Gavin Rossdale's solo album Wanderlust

Katy covers crooner Bing Crosby's classic White Christmas

2009

After 3OH!3 supported her on the Teenage Dreams tour, Katy featured in a remix of their single Starstrukk

Katy covers Sam Sparro's Black and Gold and MGMT's Electric Feel for Radio 1's Live Lounge

Katy was a featured artist on hip hop legend Timbaland's single If We Ever Meet Again

2010

California Gurls features another hip hop megastar, Snoop Dogg

E.T. is remixed by Kanye West

Say what

on simon cowell

" I love sitting next to Simon. He is a big flirt and also a very smart man. "

on voicing smurfette

" I'm going to be Smurfette; I'm so excited! I've never seen an episode, because my parents wouldn't let me. "

on her live performances

" I just really want to raise the bar. Touring is no longer an ordinary thing where you play an instrument in jeans and a T-shirt. It has some pizzaz these days, and I'm definitely bringing the pizzaz with a lot of bells and whistles. The show has a Broadway feel to it. It's got a storyline that's going to be very interesting, kind of loosely based on my life, but a cartoon version. "

on marriage

> I think you can have it all. You just have to work really hard, because great things don't come easily. Everyone's been told that marriage is hard work, and it is: You have to make time for the things you love.

on her teenage crush

> Zack Morris from Saved by the Bell was a definite crush and still is. He is really hot. It's my dream to meet him some day.

on lady gaga

> I saw her on the American Music Awards, and I was like, 'You're an animal of another kind, and we need you!' She's amazing. She's an entertainer, a visual artist. And her lyrics do mean things when you actually break them down.

Wordsearch

Z	W	K	J	T	B	N	P	W	G	M	H	S	J	C	A
R	W	E	U	E	T	C	L	M	T	O	U	Y	U	A	O
X	Y	W	C	E	H	W	B	O	E	J	V	G	F	L	O
F	F	R	J	N	E	Y	Y	D	E	E	Q	H	J	I	F
A	N	N	P	A	M	Z	T	H	E	S	M	U	R	F	S
C	O	X	L	G	A	X	R	K	I	S	S	E	D	O	M
T	V	J	H	E	T	S	Z	M	E	H	Q	C	M	R	D
O	L	V	V	A	R	M	F	N	U	A	X	T	X	N	P
R	N	C	P	T	I	X	Q	Z	X	A	A	O	J	I	Y
B	A	K	P	Q	X	K	R	U	S	S	E	L	L	A	H
U	U	F	I	R	E	W	O	R	K	N	R	N	C	D	U
K	F	D	E	L	M	O	W	V	D	W	B	J	P	D
L	S	C	G	P	U	R	R	K	B	S	H	I	W	C	S
J	F	P	G	I	X	Q	L	N	U	G	X	R	G	E	O
K	G	X	S	A	N	T	A	B	A	R	B	A	R	A	N
M	L	F	T	S	E	Z	M	L	K	W	D	S	E	N	G

California   Elmo   Purr

Russell   Hudson   The Smurfs

Teenage   Firework   The Matrix

Santa Barbara   Kissed   X Factor

Answers on page 58

Live Performances

Live performances are very important to Katy - something she enjoys, but also something she takes very seriously.

hello katy!

Her first worldwide solo tour was in 2009, the Hello Katy! tour, which promoted the album 'One Of The Boys''. The stage shows were colourful extravaganzas, filled with two of Katy's obsessions, fruit and cats. She got to help design the costumes for the show, creating the looks with someone who usually works with Madonna.

california dreams

Katy's Second tour, the California Dreams Tour started in February 2011. Katy said about it when she announced it on Twitter "I hope that it's going to engage all of your senses: sight, sound, smell, taste, touch." The look is like a crazy kid's party- giant lollipops, colourful outfits and oversized stairs.

Fashion

After a strict upbringing, anyone would want to have a little fun with their clothes and experiment with different looks, and Katy is no different.

Of course, as an artist, it's important for Katy to look great on stage and during interviews, but we get the impression that Katy loves dressing up all the time. She's not one of those people who like to slob around in a tracksuit on their day off, and we love her quirky sense of style that's usually got a bit of vintage inspiration and always stands out from the crowd. Here are a few of our fav looks...

christmas cracker

Fur trimmed red satin is really only a look you can get away with for a couple of weeks each year. Let hope Katy's been a good girl and she got all the presents she asked for.

glitterball ballerina

You might have worn a tutu at ballet class, but we don't remember them being anything like this! Pink tulle tutu with sparkly leotard top - just the thing for practising your plie.

cookie crumbles

Another sweet treat based dress, this time skintight latex and chocolate chip cookies – who are we to argue?

roll up roll up

All the fun of the fair, or the circus – Katy is still rocking this ring leader outfit – who else could pull off blue glitter high-waisted hotpants?

sweet as candy

Mmm, delicious! As well as being a great little dress, this choice looks good enough to eat. Well, if Katy gets peckish halfway through the performance, she knows where to go for a sugar rush.

glam it up

This long evening dress shows that Katy can do red carpet glamour with ease. The thigh high split manages to give this gown a bit of edge.

Famous Friends

With her enthusiastic personality, Katy is one of those people who seem to make friends easily - people just love being around her. And because of that she's made quite a few good famous friends along the way. Here are a few of her FBFs

mark jacobs

rihanna

Rihanna

Katy has described Rihanna as a 'cool chick', and the two have holidayed together in Rihanna's home island of Barbados

Jessie J

Katy asked the Essex girl to support her on her California Dreams tour

Marc Jacobs

Katy is a fan of designer Marc Jacobs creations (especially his bags), and so it-s no surprise to see the two of them happily posing for pictures when they meet – usually at one of the fashion week parties.

Russell Brand

Well he is her husband, but first and foremost, the two are great friends, and never find themselves with nothing to talk about.

Perez Hilton

Katy and the celebrity blogger are often seen together and Katy was a surprise guest at his birthday party on 2010

Crossword

ACROSS

1. Katy's favourite animal (3)

4. Katy starred as herself in this classic US cartoon The ? (8)

6. Katy's middle name, also the Queen of England (9)

8. Katy was a guest judge on the X ? (6)

10. Country where Katy got married (5)

11. Katy and Russell are Mr & Mrs ? (5)

12. Breakthrough single, I ? a Girl (6)

14. This single was remixed by Kanye West (2)

15. Katy's catty new perfume (4)

16. This flamboyant star was one of Katy's heroes, Freddie ? (7)

17. Katy listened to a lot of this style of music when growing up (6)

18. This lipbalm is often thrown on stage when Katy sings I Kissed A Girl (9)

DOWN

1. Her home state on the west coast of America (10)

2. Featured artist on California Gurls - hip hop legend (5,4)

3. Katy almost appeared on this children's TV show? Street (6)

4. Blue cartoon character Katy provided the voice for (9)

5. One of Katy's favourite vegetables (9)

7. One of Katy's musical idols ? Morissette (6)

9. ? Dreams, Katy's second album (7)

13. She wrote this song for husband Russell Brand (8)

Answers on page 58

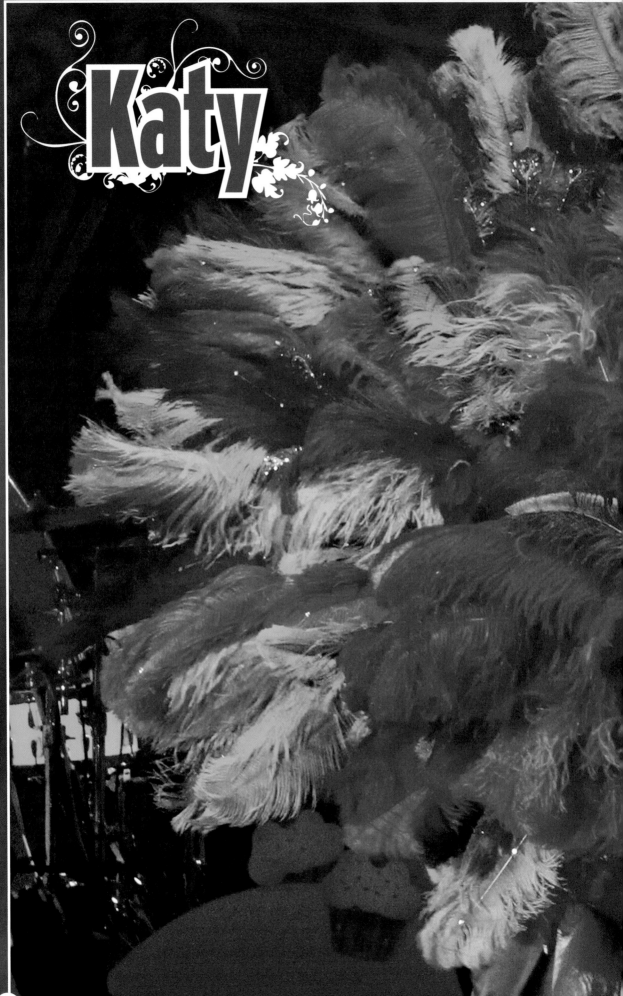

Katy

Influences

Katy has listened to lots of musical styles in her life, and that has made her more open to taking inspirations from lots of different people, from gospel to Italian opera, hip hop to rock.

But, there are a few themes that run through her influences - strong women, flamboyant performers and great song writing. Here are few of her favourites:

Alanis Morissette

At her most well-known in the 90s, Alanis Morisette sang about broken relationships and tough emotions. Katy has said that she wants to be an Alanis Morisette for a new generation, helping people express feelings that they can't normally explain.

Freddie Mercury / Queen

Katy has always said that Freddy Mercury was and is her biggest influence, on both performance and lyrics. She pays tribute to the man and his band by regularly covering their tracks during gigs, and she has even dressed up as Freddie at a fancy dress party – moustache and everything!

Cyndi Lauper

The 80s star behind hit single "Girls Just Wanna Have Fun" is someone Katy looks up to and would like to have a similar career too.

Mika

Katy first met the energetic singer before he was famous and took him out to LA to meet all her friends and colleagues. She thinks he's a lot like Freddie Mercury, but that they could never work together or it would be a circus - roll up roll up!

cyndi lauper

alanis morissette

mika

Life as a Wife

When Katy Perry turned up to film a guest appearance in the film 'Get Him To The Greek' in the summer of 2008, little did she know that she would be meeting her future husband on set.

Her scenes in the film were eventually cut, but a year later, after meeting up again at the MTV music awards, Katy and Russell started dating, Katy says that to get his attention, she threw a water bottle at Russell, but be warned girls, this doesn't always work when trying to get a man!

The couple then began officially dating, with Katy wearing a West Ham (Russell's favourite football team) basque to an award ceremony, and the couple going on holiday with Katy's parents.

The couple became engaged on holiday in India later that year, after Russell proposed while they were on top of an elephant watching a firework display. Maybe this is why Katy's song Firework is dedicated to him?

They married in October 2010, again in India, in a traditional Hindu ceremony.

Katy has said that in Russell, she has found a male version of herself, and the couple have plenty in common. They both love cats, tweeting and taking a lot of time to get ready.

While both Katy and Russell are very busy with their careers, they are working hard at spending time as a married couple, and Katy openly speaks about wanting children someday - maybe this is the next project she'll be working on? They'd certainly be good looking kids with those two as parents.

10 things...

... you didn't know about Katy ...

alanis
morissette

1 Katy's real name is Katheryn Elizabeth Hudson, but she thought that Katy Hudson sounded too similar to (actress) Kate Hudson, so she decided to work under the name Katy Perry (her mother's maiden name).

2 Katy's cat is called Kitty Purry.

3 Fans have taken to throwing cherry Chapstick at Katy when she performs *I Kissed A Girl* on stage.

4 Katy has landed the role of Smurfette's voice in the new Smurfs movie.

5 Her parents were so religious, she was only allowed to listen to gospel music growing up, and once got into trouble for singing Alanis Morissette's *Ironic* in the school playground.

6 Katy is a natural blonde.

7 She has the word 'Jesus' tattooed on her left wrist.

8 Katy's new perfume line is called Purr.

9 On her album, 'One of the Boys' Katy Perry wrote or co-wrote every song.

10 In 2009 while working on a magazine shoot, Katy Perry had a chimp on set, which peed all over her and forced her to take a shower in the middle of the shoot.

katy hudson

tattoo

Missing lyrics

Can you find the missing Katy Perry lyric?

❝ You could travel the world / but nothing come close to the

> **1** _____ ❞

❝ Glitter all over the room /

Pink **2** _____ in the pool ❞

❝ Us girls we are so **3** _____ /

Soft skin, red lips, so kissable ❞

❝ We used to be just like twins, so in sync / The same energy

now's a dead **4** _____ ❞

❝ You don't have to feel like a waste of space / You're original,

cannot be **5** _____ ❞

❝ I saw a spider, I didn't scream / Cause I can belch the

6 _____ just double dog me ❞

You think I'm pretty / without any make-up on /

You think I'm funny when I tell the /

❝ **7** _____ wrong ❞

Answers on page 58

spot the difference

Can you spot 5 differences between these image of Katy Perry on stage?

Answers on page 59

Favourite Things

tv shows: the office (american version)

food: mushrooms and fruit

drink: tea and juice

inspirational peope: jesus and ghandi

singer: freddy mercury

song: killer queen
by queen

colour: blue

film: romeo and juliet

sweets: candy

animal: cats

song she wrote:
firework

book: all you need to know about
the music business

20 questions

1 Katy was born and raised in this California Town

2 Katy's real name is?

3 Why did she change her name?

4 Raised by strict parents, this is one of the only styles of music Katy listened to when growing up

5 Katy's perfume will have you feline groovy

6 Katy often gets mistaken for this actress; in fact many people think they are sisters

7 In which country did Russell Brand propose to Katy?

8 What did Blender Magazine say Katy was in 2004?

9 Who mentioned Katy in a 2007 radio interview, bringing her to the public's attention?

10 Which US soap did Katy appear in (as herself) in 2008?

11 What is the name of Katy's Dad?

12 In which city was Katy a guest judge for the X Factor in 2010?

13 Which puppet did Katy duet with, with the song being cut from the show?

14 Which blue character did Katy voice for a 2011 film?

15 Katy met Russell while filming which feature film?

16 What is the name of Katy's Mum?

17 What musical style did Katy briefly study?

18 What starsign is Katy?

19 Which singer and friend of Katy sadly missed her wedding?

20 What was the name of Katy's 2011 word tour?

Katy's Hair

It might be hard to believe but Katy is a natural blonde, she hides it well under a variety of different dyes and wigs. She really sees her hair as an important part of the Katy Perry 'look', and because of that her hair changes a lot. Here are a few of her looks – some more successful than others!

Blue Monday

Katy does like to experiment with colour and she's tried bright blue in a couple of shades now. We're not really sure if we like it or not, but respect to Katy for trying it out in the first place – not sure we'd be brave enough for that!

Big, bouncy curls

This is the look we love to see Katy rocking. Long hair, softly curled at the ends gives Katy an old-school glamour that's perfect for the red carpet – we like!

High Ponytail

With her glossy hair scraped back into this high ponytail Katy looks stylish and relaxed - and it means she shows off her gorgeous face properly. Extensions give the ponytail extra swooshing ability. This look should be avoided if you have a round face.

Feline Groovy

Dark soft waves with just a few streaks of colour are ok, but we love the addition of the floral cat ears - just puurfect!

She Bangs

This short fringe has got a bit of vintage inspiration behind it, and while it definitely works on stage, it can look a little severe in real life. Though, if you're Katy Perry, you could probably get away with any style you like - jealous, us?

Awards

Awards are always a big part of anyone's career, and Katy has managed to be successful in all types of award ceremonies, from Teen Choice Awards, to the Brit awards, showing that she is an artist who is appreciated by the fans as well as the critics. To date Katy has been nominated for over 150 awards worldwide, and won almost 50. Here is our pick of some of her most important wins so far...

2008

MTV Europe Awards: Best New Act

2009

Brit Awards: Best International Female

People's Choice Award: Favourite Pop Song (I Kissed A Girl)

TV Guys Choice Awards: Best Siren

2010

Cosmopolitan Ultimate Women Of The Year Awards: Ultimate Star International Music

MTV Europe Awards: Best Video (California Gurls)

Teen Choice Awards: Choice Music Single (California Gurls)

Teen Choice Awards: Choice Summer Song (California Gurls)

2011

Nickelodeon's Kids' Choice Awards: Favourite Female Singer

People's Choice Award: Favourite Female Artist

People's Choice Award: Favourite Internet Sensation

A-Z of KP

A American Idol - Katy was a guest judge on this show in 2010

B *One of the Boys* - Katy's first pop album

C *California Gurls* - first single from Teenage Dreams album

D Dual citizenship - since marrying, Katy is planning to have both British and American passports

E Elephant - Russell proposed to Katy on top of one of these in India

F *Firework* - one of Katy's more explosive hits

G Gym Class Heroes - Katy's ex-Travis McCoy is lead singer in this band

H Hudson - Katy's real last name

I I Kissed A Girl - Katy's breakthrough hit

J Jitterbug - Kay trained in this dance when she was younger

K Keith - Katy's Dad

L Lip salve - fans throw cherry Chapstick at Katy when she sings *I Kissed A Girl*

M Madonna mentioned Katy on a radio programme in 2007

N Next Big Thing - Blender magazine said this of Katy in 2004

O Opera - Katy studied Italian opera for a time at college

P Purr - the name of Katy's new perfume

Q Q Magazine - Katy has been a cover star for the music magazine a couple of times

R Russell Brand - Katy and English actor Russell married in India

W World record – I Kissed A Girl earned Katie the record, Best Start on the US Digital Chart by a Female Artist

X X Factor – Katy was a guest judge on the talent show in 2010

Y The Young and the Restless – US soap Katy appeared in as herself in 2008

Z Zooey Deschanel – Katy and the US actress are often mistaken for each other

S Santa Barbara – Katy's hometown in sunny California

T The Smurfs – new film in which Katy is the voice of Smurfette

U Unplugged – Katy recorded an acoustic album in 2009

V Vintage – Katy loves using older influences in her styles

Quiz answers

20 Questions about Katie Perry - page 50

1. Santa Barbara
2. Katheryn Elizabeth Hudson
3. Because Katy Hudson sounded too much like actress, Kate Hudson
4. Gospel
5. Purr
6. Zooey Deschanel
7. India
8. The Next Big Thing
9. Madonna
10. The Young and The Restless
11. Keith
12. Dublin
13. Elmo from Sesame Street
14. Smurfette
15. Get Him To The Greek
16. Mary
17. Italian Opera
18. Libra
19. Rihanna
20. Californian Dreams

Find the missing lyric - page 42

1 'golden coast' from California Girls
2 'flamingos' from Last Friday Night
3 'magical' from I Kissed a Girl
4 'battery' from Hot N Cold
5 'replaced' from Firework
6 'alphabet' from One Of The Boys
7 'punch line' from teenage Dreams

Crossword - page 33

ACROSS
1 Cat
4 Simpsons
6 Elizabeth
8 Factor
10 India
11 Brand
12 Kissed
14 E.T.
15 Purr
16 Mercury
17 Gospel
18 Chapstick

DOWN
1 California
2 Snoop Dogg
3 Sesame
4 Smurfette
5 Mushrooms
7 Alanis
9 Teenage
13 Firework

Spot the difference - page 44

Wordsearch - page 24

Z	W	K	J	T	B	N	P	W	G	M	H	S	J	C	A
R	W	E	U	E	T	C	L	M	T	O	U	Y	U	A	O
X	Y	W	C	E	H	W	B	O	E	J	V	G	F	L	O
F	F	R	J	N	E	Y	Y	D	E	E	Q	H	J	I	F
A	N	N	P	A	M	Z	T	H	E	S	M	U	R	F	S
C	O	X	L	G	A	X	R	K	I	S	S	E	D	O	M
T	V	J	H	E	T	S	Z	M	E	H	Q	C	M	R	D
O	L	V	V	A	R	M	F	N	U	A	X	T	X	N	P
R	N	C	P	T	I	X	Q	Z	X	A	A	O	J	I	Y
B	A	K	P	Q	X	K	R	U	S	S	E	L	L	A	H
U	U	F	I	R	E	W	O	R	K	N	R	N	C	D	U
K	F	D	E	L	M	O	W	V	D	V	W	B	J	P	D
L	S	C	G	P	U	R	R	K	B	S	H	I	W	C	S
J	F	P	G	I	X	Q	L	N	U	G	X	R	G	E	O
K	G	X	S	A	N	T	A	B	A	R	B	A	R	A	N
M	L	F	T	S	E	Z	M	L	K	W	D	S	E	N	G

59

Where's Katy?